PIPPA

The Cheetah and Her Cubs

PIPPA

The Cheetah and Her Cubs

JOY ADAMSON

Harcourt, Brace & World, Inc., New York

Printed in Great Britain

Hardbound edition ISBN 0-15-262125-3

Library edition ISBN 0-15-262126-1

First American edition

One day a very small cheetah cub lost her mother. Pippa was all alone in a wild part of Kenya. She would not have lived many days if Major Dunkey had not found her. He took her home, and she became his children's pet.

But now the Dunkeys were going to England, and as they could not take a cub with them, they asked me to adopt her. Of course, I said "yes".

The first time I met Pippa she was having lunch in a restaurant with the Dunkeys.

Not long afterwards she travelled with me by car to a place near the sea, and as I was afraid that she might run away and get lost, I had a harness made for her and attached a very long nylon lead to it. She loved the sands but at first was rather suspicious of the water.

When she was not exploring the countryside, she played in a wire enclosure. Her favorite toy was an old tire.

Plainly, she was used to living with human beings, but we all agreed that she would have a happier life if she were to grow up to be a wild cheetah—although it was not going to be easy for her to revert to the exciting and dangerous life of an animal living in the bush.

After some weeks, Pippa and I went to the Meru Game Reserve, where we set up a camp that was to become her home.

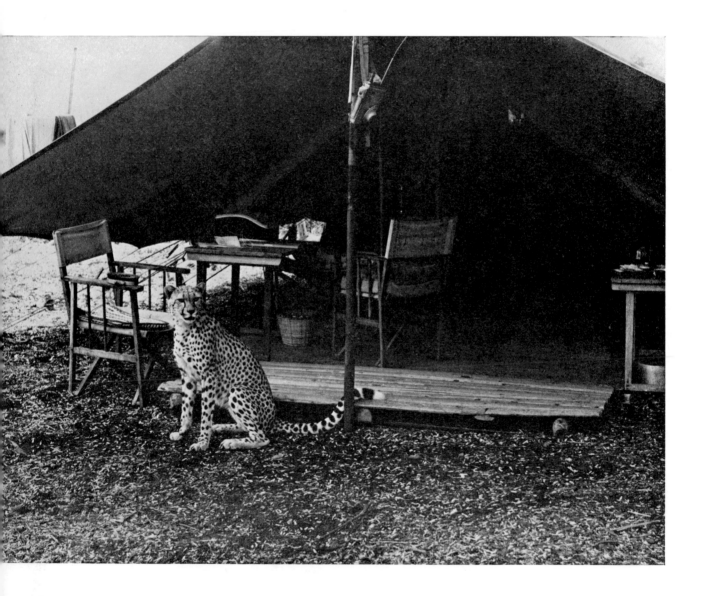

She loved to get high up on the branch of a tree.

One day George, my husband, who was camping twelve miles away, came over to see Pippa. Here they are together.

When I felt quite sure that she would not get lost I took off her harness and lead. Away she went jumping across the river.

For a moment I wondered if she would ever return, but I trusted her, and I was right, for later she came back and joined

the Game Scout and myself, who were waiting for her in
the bush

To reward her, I gave her some meat.

Afterwards she retrieved a football, a game she had invented herself.

Pippa loved standing in high places, for they gave her not only a good view of her surroundings but also suitable sites to mark her territory by leaving her droppings.

Here she is on an anthill, on a rock, and up a tree.

As the months passed, Pippa became more and more independent. She learned to kill and to feed herself; she would go off on her own for as long as three days on end, and I discovered that she was keeping company with a beautiful dark cheetah. All this made me very happy since there was now no doubt that she was going wild, and doing so without losing touch with me, even when she no longer needed the food I gave her.

One day when Pippa came back into camp, she had a surprise, for inside a new enclosure she saw a little leopard cub, called Taga.

Like Pippa, Taga had lost her mother. She had been found and looked after by a friend who had then given her to me.

I wondered what Pippa would think of Taga, and I paid a great deal of attention to her so that she should not feel jealous. I was pleased when she went up to the wire and gave a friendly purr.

The little leopard had lots of toys. She loved playing with them and doing acrobatics on the wire of her enclosure.

She was a delightful cub, and I was very worried when, at six weeks old, she became ill. I took her eighty miles by car to be treated by a vet, but she died on the twenty-third of December, and that year we had a very sad Christmas.

Two months later I saw that Pippa was going to have cubs. This was very exciting. Unfortunately I had to go to England

just then for the Royal Command Performance of *Born Free,* to which I had been summoned. While I was in London, I received a cable telling me that the litter had been born. I flew back at once, and soon after I arrived in camp Pippa came to greet me; then she led me to her nursery, where I saw three lively little cubs.

Until the rains came, I visited the family every day, but soon the ground was flooded and made moving very difficult. When at last the bush dried up, Pippa came to camp and ate ravenously, but she seemed in no hurry to go back to her cubs. Day after day I searched for them, but I never found them, so I think they must have been killed.

After these sad events I was thrilled when in the late summer I noticed that Pippa was going to have a second litter. I wondered whether, when they were born, she would hide them from me or again guide me to them. Then one day she led me to a bush, and inside it I saw four little cubs.

This is what they looked like when they were twelve days old.

Whenever the cubs messed up their nursery, Pippa took them, dog fashion, one by one by the scruff of the neck to a new place.

The cubs grew very quickly as you can see by these photos, taken when they were eighteen days, thirty days, and five weeks old.

I gave the cubs names: Whity, Tatu, Mbili and Dume—he was the only male.

They suckled Pippa.

To help her with her feeding problems, I took meat to her, and it was not long before the cubs joined her in eating it. I then introduced them to drinking water. At first they were very suspicious of the bowl, but they soon got used to lapping out of it.

Pippa was very affectionate and used to lick the cubs all over.

Little Dume, as the only male, felt that he should protect the pride. He often sat by his mother guarding her.

While still very young, the cubs lived through many dangers. There was a bush fire, and when the rains came, there were floods, but Pippa looked after her family with such care that no harm came to them.

It was in December when I noticed that Dume was very lame. I radio-called a vet in Nairobi, who flew to our camp. After we had caught Dume and given him an anaesthetic, the vet decided that he must fly him to Nairobi and examine him more thoroughly. Two days later I had a message to say that the X-ray showed that Dume had two broken legs, but that the bones should knit quickly. It was therefore a great shock when I heard that he had got infected with distemper in Nairobi and had died. Ever since he had been caught and taken away, Pippa and the other cubs had been very distressed.

As soon as they were old enough, Pippa began to teach
Mbili, Tatu and Whity to climb trees; sometimes they balanced
high up on a branch, and sometimes they fell off.

Like their mother they also loved playing on anthills,

and everything I provided them with, cartons, bowls, baskets,
and even milk cans, suggested some new game.

The cubs were six months old when I observed that Whity could not keep pace with the others and was dragging a leg. Like Dume she must have injured her legs when jumping off a tree. Cheetahs are not built for tree climbing and acquired this habit only after we humans had deprived them of their natural home—the open plains—and forced them to live in more wooded country. In order to look around, they learned to climb trees, but they often break their legs when jumping down. These injuries partly account for the high death rate among cheetahs. I was horrified to see how lame Whity was and decided to catch her and bring her into camp. The only way I could do this was by first starving her and then giving her some doped meat. After she had eaten it, she became very sleepy, and with the help of the vet, who had flown in to examine her, we managed to carry her to camp and to bandage her leg.

They told me that she would take a little time to get well, and advised me to keep her in an enclosure to prevent her from taking too much exercise. Poor Whity, she hated being shut up and used to pace angrily up and down behind the wire, calling to her family.

It was a great day when she was quite well again and I was able to open the door of the enclosure and see her bound out to rejoin her family who were waiting nearby.

Pippa now moved her family to a sand patch by a pool.

They had a wonderful time racing round and exploring the bush.

Pippa watched them from her seat on a high branch.

It was now that she began to teach them to hunt. Sometimes when they came home, they were so tired that they just lay down on the road.

Often, two of them would have a tug of war over a piece of meat, or have fun retrieving a piece of skin.

From this time onward Pippa and the cubs only came to camp about once a fortnight to say "Hello" to us and have an extra meal.

Every day Pippa widened their territory, and I often had to walk many miles to see them.

It was clear to me that their mother was soon going to leave the cubs to lead their own independent lives.

Mbili had been the skinniest of the cubs but later became the handsomest of the family. Then one day I was horrified to see that she had a badly injured eye. It was almost closed. I radio-called the vet, and for the second time he flew out to help us, accompanied by his wife.

It was very difficult to catch Mbili and to give her a drug to make her sleepy, but in the end we succeeded, and the Harthoorns treated her eye.

It was not long before Mbili was well again. Her eye healed perfectly.

Pippa left Whity, Tatu and Mbili, and I did not see any of them for some time. Then one day Pippa returned. She made me follow her into the bush and showed me...her third family.

I was very happy to see that Pippa was capable of having cubs so easily. This proved that her rehabilitation had been a complete success, for cheetahs do not breed well in captivity and their numbers also decline alarmingly in their wild state.

My hope is that by observing the lives and habits of wild cheetahs we may be able to learn how to help preserve this lovely species.